OVERCOMING CHALLENGES,
AGAINST ALL ODDS

OVERCOMING CHALLENGES, AGAINST ALL ODDS

DORIS GONZALEZ

Contents

Dedication

I dedicate this book to my **family**.

To my loving husband Erik, my three sons Carlos, Andrew and Evan who are my life (Two are my natural born sons, one is my step-son) my parents, my brother Eddie, his wife and my two nieces, My grandmother and all of my cousins.

I dedicate this to my best friend and sister from another mister, Gigi. And to life long friends Liz, Juan Carlos, Blanca, Ruby, Sonya, Vivian, Addie and Maribel.

I dedicate this book to my mini-golden doodle, Roswell Picadillo. He is truly loved as if he were my fourth son. He will never know, how much he helped me through the toughest parts of my life.
And lastly but not least, to a thriving female leader who inspired me to write my story,
Eli King Thompson.

Copyright

CHAPTER 1

Newark

Chapter One- Newark

It was a Good Friday on April 20th, 1973 and I was born in Newark, New Jersey in Beth Israel Hospital. It was a Good Friday because I was born, but also because it was the Friday before Easter Sunday and it is considered a holy day in the Catholic and Christian religions.

My mother was just 22 years old and my father was 29 years of age when I was born. My mom had migrated into the United States from the Dominican Republic in 1969 on her 18th birthday. My dad was 17 when he fled communist Cuba in 1963, just a few years after the 1959 Castro revolution. The day he left his native country, he told no one.

Not even his parents. He and a handful of other friends sailed in a small vessel with the excuse that they were going fishing. It would be 50 years before he returned to his homeland. He swore, he would not return until Fidel Castro was gone.

4

As fate would have it, he returned to Cuba in 2016 along with my mom and I, the day Fidel Castro passed away.

CHILDHOOD

I had a wonderful childhood in New Jersey. My family owned a multi-family home, where my paternal grandparents lived in the first floor, my dad, mom, brother and I lived on the second floor, and we were landlords to families in the third floor, and in the basement apartment.

My mother was a home maker, and my father was a sales professional for Canada Dry bottling company. We were a middle class family and both my brother and I went to Catholic Private school, St. Michaels School in Newark, NJ.

Across the street from our home, my maternal grandparents owned a multi-family home as well. My oldest uncle lived with his wife Josephine on the first floor for a while, until they purchased their own home and moved farther away. My grandparents were landlords to Tenants on the other floors.

Next door to my grandparents home, lived my youngest uncle, his wife and soon to be two young sons. My brother and I were very close to those two young cousins growing up. I was the oldest, but the other three children were closer in age. After a few years, they too moved and purchased their own multi-family home in Kearny, NJ.

I have so many fond memories of the holidays with my family. Christmas was an epic holiday. Thanksgiving was also wonderful, but

Christmas time as a child was magical. At school, we would sing Christmas carols for what seemed like two months. We had an annual Christmas show, where all children played a part and sang even more Christmas carols. The halls were decked, and the spirit of Christmas was palpatible.

At home, all immediate family and extended cousins would gather at abuela's house for Christmas Eve dinner, and at midnight, all of the gifts would magically appear inside huge black garbage bags. Throughout many years extended family came to join us as well. We had second cousins and great aunts and uncles join too. The first cousins were my brother and I, and our cousins Aldwin and Edrick. Boy were we blessed. One year in 1984, I received two Cabbage patch Dolls, along with a plethora of Barbie dolls, my brother received the GI Joe headquarters with a ton of action figures , My cousins Aldwin and Edrick had Castle Grayskull and action figures and action animals from the He-Man, Master of the Universe franchises. We were on top of the world, with no worries at all.

We had a blast and it wasn't always during Christmas. Our parents would go on dates on Friday nights and leave the four cousins with Grandma and Grandpa for the weekend. My maternal grandfather wasn't too thrilled. He cherished his peace and quiet, (looking back now, who could blame him) but our grandmother loved having us around all the time. Even though we were a rowdy bunch, they loved our company, and we loved our grandmother's cooking, our grandfather's sense of humor and their love.

The first six years of my life I was an only child. I was the only granddaughter and the only niece. Things were pretty cool.

My younger brother was born in 1978. At first I didn't appreciate him, as I was only six years old and it seemed my entire life prior to this point, life seemed to revolve around me. All of a sudden all of that had changed. Soon after the initial shock, his cute smile and adorable gestures, made it so easy to love my brother. I am so grateful that I share our familial DNA and life experience with such an amazing and wonderful human being.

In the fall of 1979, I attended first grade at St. Michael's School in Newark, NJ. I remember that although I was born in the United States I was not fluent in English. In the home, we mostly spoke Spanish. Luckily, my first grade teacher Ms. Echenique was bilingual, and I was able to adapt very quickly. Today I am fluent in both English and Spanish.

I thrived in St.Michael's School. I made many friends who I am still friends with today. Marcy was my best friend since first grade. Thanks to social media, we are still great friends today and have shared many meals and visits as adults. Our Principal Linda Cerino, is my current friend on Facebook! I made life long connections, and received a stellar elementary school education and owe so much of who I am to that institution.

Academically it was great, but also there were many extra curricular events and groups. In Fifth grade I was a Cheerleader. I had so much fun from try outs, to practice, to participating in local parades down loomfield Avenue.

I remember having my first crush. A tall green eyed basketball player named Wilver.

The population in the school was very diverse. Hence why I never felt different, or even was aware that different ethnicities really existed. I guess I never gave it too much thought. In that school there was a large population of Puerto Ricans, Blacks, Whites, Italians, and we all got along. We were all just kids learning, and having a fun childhood experience for the most part. I felt at home especially since I was bi-racial and multi-cultural.

The 80s were great. From Maddona and Michael Jackson on MTV to Saturday morning cartoons, to great movies like the Karate Kid. Ironically Karate Kid was about a kid from Newark, NJ that moved to another state, and experienced some challenges in the new school. Little did I know, I may be experiencing something like that in the near future.

At some point in 1980, my paternal grandparents moved to Miami. Being Cuban, they had a lot of friends in Miami and were better acclimated to the weather and the culture.

From 1980 to 1984, my parents, brother and I would vacation in Miami. The weather was nice, and the food was amazing.

Towards the end of 1984, my parents stated that they would be selling our house in New Jersey and were building two additions to our house in Miami. My maternal grandparents would be selling their New Jersey home as well and would be moving to Miami with us. My dad and maternal grandmother were purchasing a business in Miami, and we would all be moving. If it sounds like a lot of change very quickly, it was. Especially for a happy, ten year old girl.

When we asked about school, my parents said there was a St. Michael's School in Miami, and that it would be exactly the same as the one in Jersey. I believed them. I had no choice, but to believe them. When the time came to arrange our travel, we went to a travel agency in the corner of our school, to purchase our tickets. There I saw Wilver the boy I had a secret crush on and he saw me. He was riding his bicycle outside the travel agency. He saw us through the glass, and he poked his head in to say hello and asked what we were doing there. I shared that my family was moving to Florida and we were purchasing our airplane tickets. We said our goodbyes. Come to think of it, that was the first time my heart was broken.

After that, my life would change from day to night.

CHAPTER 2

Miami

Chapter Two- Miami

In any given moment you can hear the Miami Sound Machine music playing in the background. Tropical percussion and drum beats were the heartbeat of Miami. In the background you could always hear some type of news media outlet. My grandparents loved watching the news on the TV or listening to it on the AM radio in Spanish. The main topic was always against the Castro regime in Cuba. Somehow the topic daily was about the plight of the Cuban people, and the politics surrounding it. Every day whether early in the morning or in the early afternoon the smell of Cuban coffee engulfed the air. As a proud republican family at the time, there was a written framed letter from Ronald Reagan addressed to my grandparents on the wall for their 50th wedding anniversary.

It was common for me to be watching MTV on the evenings and on the weekends. I didn't have any friends yet, and my parents were over-protective. Included in the cable television in the 80s in Miami, was a channel called the BOX. There were videos of hip hop and urban music. I enjoyed watching both of those very much. I've always had a very diverse taste in music. I loved rock, pop and hip hop. I was never much of a country music fan. Today, in 2024 I love Taylor Swift...though I digress.

My family owned a bakery/cafeteria in Homestead, FL even though we lived in Miami. It was about a 45 minute drive south and it was called Capuccino Bakery. There was always cake, pastelitos, cuban bread and delicious food readily available at the house from the cafeteria. All this in addition to my grandparents cooking. Good food was definitely part of our culture.

The bakery was open 7 days a week, and it was a great source of stress for my family. It was open 7 days a week, difference in leadership direction among my family, employee issues and distance all contributed to the stress. They would sell it a few years later in 1990.

In the middle of the sixth grade I transferred schools and was enrolled in St. Michael School the Archangel in Miami. The school looked different than the one in New Jersey. The school had a different vibe. Most of the children there were very tight knit. They had grown up together, and had already made many memories together. I knew there was something very different, although I couldn't pinpoint what it was yet. And then it hit me, everyone looked similar, except for me. I was dark skinned with curly dark hair and everyone else was fair skinned. Most kids were descendants from Cuba or Colombia but had European ancestry. I stood out like a sore thumb.

Some of my classmates had been together since the first grade, and possibly never had an afro-latina in any of their classes. I was an outsider, they didnt know who I was. Many of the students embraced me and were very kind. Others saw me as different, and would laugh behind my back and make me feel unwelcomed.

I remember the Beastie Boys had a hit song called Grease Monkey in the mid to late 80s. Some kids would sing that to me as I would pass by. As though to imply I was a monkey because my skin color was brown. I had only been alive 10 to 11 years, but that was one of my unhappiest times. I was homesick. It would ease up and get better.

Luckily, this was temporary. I had enough self esteem to compartmentalize the change of moving states, losing friends, and now being made fun of at school. In the grand scheme of my life, this would only amount to a couple of years. Inspite the negative, I was blessed to meet my best friend who also was enrolled in 6th grade mid year. Her name was Gigi, we were 11 years of age and were immediate best friends. We were both different. I was of a darker complexion and came from New Jersey and Gigi, had been in public school her entire life before then. Just a few weeks prior, I was happy, a cheerleader, unaware that kids could be cruel with other kids. That changed. But I overcame.

After 8th grade graduation, Gigi, myself, and about 75 percent of the other kids in our grade went to St. Brendan Highschool also in Miami. During the ninth grade, my grades started to decline especially in Science and Math. By then, I learned to adapt to the surroundings, the culture and the people. As a 15 year old ninth grader in St. Brendan, I met a few more life long friends. One of which was Liz. Her mom passed away of cancer during that year. I was able to go to the hospital and spend time with my friend while she was going through this with her family. I also became friends with Juan Carlos. He and Liz dated for a while. He would join us to all of the Sweet fifteen parties that year. Although he went to an all boys private school next door, he seemed to be at all of our school's events. Jc had a best friend named Erik. Because my parents didn't allow me to leave the house much, I spent a lot of time on the phone with my friends. JC would tell me all about his friend Erik. The girls he dated and the trips he would take with his family. Erik seemed to go to a Marriott Hotel in Marco Island Florida a lot, and sometimes would take his girl friend. JC and I would remain friends. One day in 1990, I got to meet Erik. He was very handsome. He had arrived in a new red sports car, he was 16 and had just graduated from Columbus Highschool early. (He skipped a grade in elementary school, attended Belen for Middle school and transferred to Columbus in the 10th grade.) I remember thinking, this is exactly the kind of guy that would never give me the time of day. He would never look at a girl like me. Exactly 20 years later, that would change. But that's another chapter.

In an effort to improve my grades, in the summer before tenth grade I went to Miami Senior High School to retake Algebra 2 and Biology. Miami High, had a different energy. It reminded me of the diversity of my elementary school in Jersey. I no longer had to try to fit in, I was able to be myself and was immediately accepted. I aced Math and Biology. I begged my parents to let me stay in Miami High and not return to St. Brendan. My grandparents did not want me to leave the catholic school. My dad was ecstatic because he no longer had to pay the monthly tuition, plus uniforms, plus books, plus raffle tickets, events and the list goes on. Miami High, had a little bit of a bad reputation among private school circles. I would later learn that many of the cocaine cowboys of the 1980s era graduated or had attended Miami High. Thank God I was oblivious to the bad reputation, I never saw a drug during my three years there, and I excelled academically and personally.

I had just one major challenge to overcome if I wanted to attend that school. Miami High was not in my school district. The school assigned to me was South Miami High, which my brother would later graduate from. However, I didn't want to leave St. Brendan just to leave. I wanted to attend Miami High. I learned that I had to take a course that was offered in Miami High, that was not offered in South Miami High in order to be allowed here. We discovered there were two classes, auto mechanic shop and the musical instrument Harp class. Alrighty then, it was decided I would take Harp for the next three years!

In Miami high, I joined Beta a service club that required a 3.0 GPA or higher to qualify to become and stay a member. I was elected as the First Vice President of Student Government, elected by the entire school population. Miami High, was a very large school. I participated in the Girls Basketball team in 10th grade (I was not good). I was in the court observer program where I went every Wednesday to the court house in the afternoons and observed live trials or trial proceedings . After six months of that, I was able to be an intern for the state attorney's office, under Janet Reno. My dream then was to become an attorney. It was a great experience. I met my first boyfriend Alex, in Miami High.

I graduated from Miami Senior High School in 1991, and enrolled in Miami Dade Community College to earn an associate degree in Law.

Today, I am friends not only with my New Jersey, St. Michaels school mates, but also with the Miami, St. Michaels school mates. Today we are all now adults, and I have gotten to know many of those students and their families. Some have grown to be excellent pillars of our society from fire fighters, to law enforcement, to teachers, to a Judge! I enjoy interacting with them weekly in a WhatsApp chat. I have also had the pleasure of attending a few mimosa brunches with a few of them.

Furthermore, today some of my closest friends graduated with me at Miami High. Most of them I met as adults planning a school reunion. Blanca, Ruby, Sonya, Addie, Vivian and Maribel are all great friends. We call ourselves The Locas. We interact in a group chat, but also make it a point to get togeher frequently throughout the year. There was another member of the Locas named Lourdes. She was vivacious and full of life. She passed away in 2020. She is missed.

Today, Gigi is still like my sister and best friend. We interact daily through text, Tik Tok sharing, and we make it a point to get together frequently. She has been with me in almost every key event of my life. What a blessing.

Wife, Mother

Chapter Three- Wife, Mother

I've been working since I was 16 years of age. At first on a part time basis, a couple of nights a week. Then slowly progressed to more hours and more days. My second Job was working for a retail store called Mervyn's in the Miami International Mall. I worked there for three years and it was a blast. There I met my second boyfriend Miguel. My BFF Gigi worked there for a time. And I met many life long friends there too. Most importantly, my third boyfriend who turned into my husband and father of my two sons.

Carlos is 2 years older than I am, and was a student of Florida International University when we met. He had just transferred from Penn State University. He was studying Engineering. Carlos was born in Guayaquil, Ecuador. He was very handsome with beautiful hair and muscular body. He was shy and introverted but a good human being.

I was 19 years of age, and at this time my parents were divorcing. After 22 years of marriage, my mother asked my dad for a divorce. Earlier in their marriage, they had issues. My dad had been unfaithful several times. My mother, had two kids, knew limited English, and suffered in silence. However, she had recently flown to the Dominican Republic with my grandparents and she ran into her first boyfriend. The same boyfriend, my grandmother did not approve of. My mother felt smitten, and alive for the first time in decades.

Before telling me what she was planning on doing, my mom arranged a professional photo shoot of her, my brother and I. It was at a store like JC Penney or Sears. We didn't even ask why dad wasn't in the picture. At that time, we didn't notice how peculiar this was. It would become clear later.

Eventually, my mother explained her predicament, and stated she would be divorcing our father and moving to the Dominican Republic. I wish I could say I was incredibly introspective or that I understood the gravity of what was occurring. I didn't. I selfishly was thinking, with my mom gone, there will be no more over protectiveness. I will be able to do whatever I want. And for a while, it was like this, I went to clubs and stayed up late many nights a week. I didn't realize how much my father was suffering because of my mom, because of my behavior and because of my brother.

But with time I realized my fourteen year old brother would not have a present mother during the most important time of his life, my father who is not emotionally mature or available would be alone, and I would not have a mother during the time that I was becoming a woman, a wife and a mother. I temporarily took a maternal role for my brother. Buying him video games and spending time with him.

My maternal grandparents moved out of the house and moved to Broward county. My father now owned a couple of movie rental stores and a Laundromat.

My home felt empty. I was unhappy there. I spent more and more time with my boyfriend Carlos in his apartment. Paying for utilities and expenses took a center stage and I left school.

In 1994, I had my first salaried corporate job at a company called PageNet, working Monday through Friday, 8am to 5pm, 40 hours per week. My salary in 1994, was $16,000 per year.

Carlos and I were married in the Coral Gables Court House on January 17, 1995. Only my mom was in attendance, she flew from the Dominican Republic to attend. We did not have a honeymoon.

Again, my life was filled with drastic change. I had to overcome, with patience and love.

On November 1, 1995 my first born came into this world in Baptist Hospital in Miami. My son Carlos, showed me how much capacity was in my heart to love. He was born at 3am, I remember not actively pushing before because I didn't want a halloween baby. After the birth of my first son, we moved to Broward county to be near my maternal grandparents. My grandparents helped to take care of my son, and soon both sons while I worked full time.

On April 11, 1997 Andrew was born in Broward county. He was such a wonderful baby. My two sons gave my grandparents a lot of joy. Especially after their daughter, the reason they moved to Florida, had moved away to the Dominican Republic, with someone they did not approve of.

Every couple of years, my mom would come and spend time with us. She would join us on trips to Disney World and would spend time with us from time to time.

It was very tough financially for a few years, but we were a family and there was a lot of love.

I would be promoted to sales and account management, and soon I would becoome the primary breadwinner. My husband seemed to be between jobs a lot. My household and my two sons were on my shoulders, and I accepted that responsibility.

After a few years of survival mode, I realized that my life had gone on a detour, and I desperately wanted to get back on track. I had dropped out of college. I wanted to earn my bachelors degree, and if I was not to become a lawyer, I wanted to expand and grow professionally. I shared my feelings with my husband. He clearly stated, my college was my kids now. I was too old to go to school, that my job was to be a working mom. I was in my twenties! I knew at that moment, that was the beginning of the end of that marriage.

I came from a broken home. I know the ramifications on the children. But I knew in my heart, that my kids and I deserved to live in the home we wanted, to have the vacations we wanted, they deserved to have a role model that could overcome adversity and challenges.

The marriage ended. To this day, Carlos is a good man and a good father. Unfortunately, our world view did not align. I will always be grateful to him, for being the father of my sons.

In between my first husband and my current life partner, I had a relationship.

He was 6 feet tall, and four years my junior. At first he seemed to worship the ground I and my sons walked on.

The relationship, had positives. I earned my Bachelors Degree. I helped him overcome cancer, through my financial support. He cared for my sons and gave them fond memories.

At the same time he was bi-polar. With many highs and many lows. He was armed with a gun and was not always medicated.

I endured a lot of stress, and a lot of embarrassment due to the behavioral illnesses he had.

That relationship ended in March of 2009. It ended peacefully. I am grateful for the good, and send him light and love whenever he crosses my mind, which is seldom.

CHAPTER 4

Life Partner

I first met Erik in 1990, when we were 16 and he had just graduated a year early. He was headed to school to Tulane University in New Orleans a few days after. Ultimately, he would only be there his Freshman year. He transfered to the University of Miami and graduated with a psychology degree in 1994. He would later earn his Masters in Educational leadership from Nova University.

In 1990, he personified everything I wanted in a partner. He was handsome, intelligent, he valued education, and had a nice sports car.

In December of 2009, our friend Juan Carlos had randomly made a post on FaceBook that changed everything. In the 80s, JC's voicemail stated- You have reached the right number at the wrong time, leave a message. It turns out that in 2009, he still had the same voicemail greeting. There was a post regarding this in the social media site. Both Erik and I posted a comment on that thread recalling how long this greeting had existed.

During this time Erik had separated from his wife and mother of his son, Evan. Erik was living with his mother in Miami. Evan was 2 1/2 years old.

Before we knew it, we were planning a group outing for February 5, 2010 to see a Hockey Panthers Game in Broward county. The plan was for JC, his girlfriend, Erik and I to attend. My sons were with their dad that weekend.

The night before the outing, I received a message that JC and his girlfriend were unable to attend, and asked if I would be ok still going with Erik. (I think they planned this..lol)

Erik and I had our first date. There were a couple of hiccups. But I knew at a soul level he was destined to be my partner. We had an amazing time. I later learned from his mom, that he stated after the date, that he thought he had found his partner.

A couple of months later he was completely divorced. We were on a five day cruise to Jamaica in March of 2010 when we received the news.

That was 14 years ago. His son Evan, was 2 and half and now he will be celebrating his 17th birthday. My two natural born sons and my step son have shared many vacations and many life experiences, and I couldn't be more grateful for our blended family.

Erik and I were married on July 1, 2012 in Mandalay Bay Resort in Las Vegas. Close family attended the wedding. My best Friend Gigi was my maid of honor. Friends Liz and Ruby were in my wedding party along with my friend Edith. JC was Erik's best man. My sons Carlos and Andrew gave me away. Evan my step son was only five years old at that time, so he didn't go to Vegas for the wedding, but he attended our vow renewal ten years later in Las Vegas.

In 2015, we purchased a four bedroom home in a gated community in south Florida after renting a couple homes in the previous few years.

22 years after my parents divorced and my mom remarried, she divorced a second time. Each marriage lasting 22 years. My mom moved back to the states and joined our home.

CHAPTER 5

Successful Career

For three decades I have excelled in a sales career. From business to business pagers, to cell phones, to HR solutions, to HCM SaaS solutions, to technology for the Insurance industry. I have been an individual contributor and a sales leader. Very few people can do well in both roles, I am one of them.

Sales can have a negative connotation. But it truly s a noble way to make a very good living.

Sales can be a way to truly serve and help businesses reach their maximum potential. Businesses employ human beings who support families and the communities they live in. Helping businesses to thrive, helps individuals, famiilies and communities. Very few careers pay well and can be so rewarding emotionally. The more a sales professional cares about the business they are serving, the higher the earning potential and success.

Although I have been an award winning sales rep of the year recipient in multiple industries since the year 2000, I have not reached a Vice President level or C level role. I started my own consulting business in 2014, in which I am a founder and CEO. But I havent been promoted to those levels in the corporate world. I have seen many start where I started , saw them leave their roles, and come back to a higher role. Because I am he main breadwinner in my household, I have taken fewer risks, hence why I have not changed companies as often as others have.

I take my work very seriously, and am emotionally vested in my customer's success. Hopefully, the consistent success will afford me a more leadership role.

I recently earned an MBA from Boston University and earned the Field Seller of the Year for 2023. All while battling cancer, but that's a future chapter.

This is a time for self reflection, and a time to manifest the next chapters of my life. Hence why I decided to write my key life events down on paper and write this book. This is a way for me to heal wounds I didn't know I had, and to help me discover what my next chapters should be.

CHAPTER 6

Vacations

One thing I love, my husband loves, and everyone in my family loves.... VACATIONS! Because we live near the Miami and Fort Lauderdale area, we are able to conveniently board Cruise ships without the need to travel to get to a port. Although, traveling to get to a port has not stopped us.

Alaska was breathtaking. The weather, the eagles, the terrain, the sea planes, the totem poles were surreal. Experiencing the culture and meeting people there was truly a great experience. Life slows down in Alaska. I really appreciate that state.

Alaska

Barcelona is an amazing city. Our family attended a Tablao, which was in a 1500s tavern in a cave like setting. We had delicious food and saw amazing performers. My mother in law, my parents and kids joined and it was a memorable event.

Monte Carlo was unforgettable. Being in the cathedral where princess Grace Kelly was interred seemed surreal. Watching my sons drinking Monaco beer and seeing my husband go into the Monte Carlo Casino and lose 150 dollars in five minutes would permanently become a part of my wonderful list of memories.

Eating delicious pizza in Sorrento, Italy with my kids and parents was heavenly. So much had transpired in our lives, and to have peace and unity be the culmination is Gods work.

Taking my step-son, parents and kids to the Colloseum in Rome was such a monumental milestone. Our family had watched the movie the Gladiator many times, and hearing my step-son yell "Are you not entertained?" in the colloseum was definitely a highlight.

Speaking of my step-son, he is a Seattle Seahawks football fan. Taking him to the Seattle stadium and going through a stadium tour was a lot of fun.

We've been to Mexico and the Bahamas many times. Cayman Islands, Jamaica, St. Lucia, are just a few of the many tropical destinations that we have been blessed to visit.

In 2021, I had the blessing to go with my mom to Hawaii. The culture, the food, the mounains, the ocean, the landscape were unforgettable. Going to the Pearl Harbor memorial, and seeing were President Barack Obama lived and went to school were truly special.

Both the west and east coast of Canada are phenomenal.

In 2016, my parents and I went to Baracoa, Cuba his birth place. I met my first cousins for the first time. I visited the home my paternal grandparents built for the first time. It had been fifty years since my dad went to his home. It was a very meaningful trip for me to go there with my father.

Dad and I in Baracoa, Cuba

In addition to travelling for work and having visited most of the US, I had a chance to travel last year to Turkey. I visited Istanbul and Kusadasi. I loved the mix of old and new. An ancient city, mixed in with new modern technology, we loved it.

Furthermore, I visited Athens and the Greek Isles. Oh my God the Food!!!!!! What an amazing experience, creating memories that will last a lifetime. That trip my friend Gigi went, my son Andrew and step son Evan went, my mom went, and because Erik was unable to go due to work, Eileen, Evan's mom joined us. We are truly a blended family with peace and respect at the very center.

Being an award winning seller has earned me trips to Costa Rica, PuertoRico, Cabo San Lucas and other tropical destinations.

Travelling and vacations are a key part of our lives, and make hard work and overcoming challenges worth it.

CHAPTER 7

Boston University

In 2021, I was 48 years old. I got the itch again. The need to get back to school itch. I felt I needed something to further expand my career and my impact to this world. I learned that Boston University had an Online MBA curriculum with the same professors of their brick and mortar school and offering the same diploma.

I gathered my transcripts, I completed my application, and I submitted a required video explaining why I wanted to earn an MBA from BU. My Strategic Sales VP Steph, was kind enough to write a letter of recommendation for me. I will always be appreciative of her.

A few months later, I received the celebratory letter, that I had been accepted to be included in the 4th OMBA cohort that started in January of 2022.

This gave me joy on many different levels. Part of my life journey, is to continue self expanding, to continue to challenge myself to grow professionally. I had such a non traditional start to secondary education, that deciding to earn my MBA and to get accepted at my age gave me immense satisfaction.

Being a part of this global community opened me up to experiences and people that I would otherwise not have met.

I have made friends from all over the world, and can be empathetic to experiences of classmates in Ukraine, in Gaza, in Africa and globally.

Setting a goal, doing the work and acheiving the goal without knowing the huge road block I would be receiving just months later, adds to my resilience and my tenacity. Having a difficult journey makes the destination that much sweeter.

The first six months were fantastic. And then my life took a dark and drastic turn. Again, the pattern of my life thus far....Joy, calm and then disruptive change. I have learned change will happen, it's how we navigate through it and learn that will bring us peace.

CHAPTER 8

Cancer Diagnosis

During the Superbowl of 2022, I got sick with Covid for the first time. I spent a week isolated in a bedroom in my home. Two years prior in December of 2020, I lost my beloved aunt Josephine to Covid. Her passing devastated my family. I loved her like a second mom. She was only 65 years of age and I will always love her. Her daughters, my cousins suffered the most, and I am here for any support they may ever need in my lifetime.

Coincidentally, after I recovered from my bout with Covid, I noticed changes in my body. My bowel cadence changed seemingly overnight. I began to think I had developed complications relating to Covid. There were rumors that folks that had had Covid, experienced changes in their bodies long term.

I made an appointment with my primary care physician. They provided me with a referral appoinment to see a GI Doctor. At this point we were in February, the appointment was set for mid April. In April I met with the GI Doctor, and they referred me to take a colonoscopy.

My symptoms persisted. The colonoscopy was scheduled for June 27, 2022. Prior to that year the recommended age to get a colonoscopy was 50 years of age. In 2022, the recommended age was lowered to 45. This was due to the increase in younger people being diagnosed with Colorectal cancer.

June 27th, came and my husband drove me to the surgical center for the procedure. He was told he would be texted when I was ready to be picked up.

I was given anesthesia and I was put under and the colonoscopy was performed.

As soon as I am awake, the doctor is next to me. I utered the words, I have cancer correct? And he said **yes.**

He proceeds to tell me he has been in touch with the chief Colorectal surgeon at Memorial Healthcare Hospital. He had already set an appointment for me to visit him within 48 hours. I was told some polyps were removed, but a tumor the size of a golf ball was malignant and near my rectum.

I can't describe the feeling of hearing you have malignant cancer and that the tumor was that large. I had a feeling before the diagnosis that it was cancer, even though I am a very positive person. I knew at that moment, my life would never be the same.

I called my husband and gave him the news. I just couldn't wait to tell him in person, I had to tell him that moment.
He was incredulous, in disbelief. He asked me what, and to repeat myself, as he thought there had to be a mistake.

He picked me up from the surgical center, and we drove home. It was a long and sad drive home. When we finally arrived, we gathered my mom and my two sons and asked for a family meeing in the family room.

I gave them the news, we all cried and cried.

I pulled my mom and husband aside, as if I was not the one that had just been diagnosed with cancer. I told them, I needed them to be stronger than ever. I explained I would get much worse before I got better, and I needed them to ensure our household kept afloat and to help me survive this. I was consoling them at first.

As it turns out my mother and husband were my rock day in and day out.

After meeting the surgeon, he explained that I did in fact have a large malignant tumor. It appeared to be slow moving and had not perforated the colon lining, and had not gone to any lymph nodes or any other organs. That day through an office procedure, I was able to see the tumor face to face. I named it Matilda. Based on what we knew then, the course of action would be 7 rounds at first, later 8 rounds of 4 drugs of chemo therapy, 25 rounds of radiation, a lower anterior resection surgery, a temporary ileostomy bag, and then six weeks later if possible a reversal surgery.

I was a new life.

The chemo portion of the process was horrible. I almost died after the first session.

A chemo session consisted of administering the chemo for five hours at the cancer center, then for the next three days, I was hooked up to a fanny pack that consistently administered the canceer drugs. The session was on Tuesday, and I would return to the cancer center on Fridays to remove the fanny pack, and receive hydration for a couple of hours.

My kids, Erik, my mom, Gigi, Eileen my step-son's mom, all did one or more sessions with me. I will always be grateful for as long as I live.

On the Friday after the first session, I blacked out in the kitchen. My son, mom and husband screamed to wake me up while calling 911. An ambulance took me to the hospital. They gave me hydration and allowed my body to strengthen. The future chemo doses were minimized by a small amount, to allow my body to tolerate the chemo.

I still had 7 more sessions to go. With every session my body became weaker. After the session I had uncontrollable diareah and vomitting. I was given medications for the nausea, and steroids for strength, but it was difficult to overcome.

During this time, I still worked part time. On chemo week I was off work and on medical leave. the in between chemo weeks, I worked fully.

The nails on my hands and feet became black. My tongue became dark. I had hyper pigmentation on my face and my hair was thinning. The chemo was killing the tumor, but it was killing the rest of me too. I developed neropathy on my hands and feet, inflamation on my entire body and felt very fatigued.

After the eight rounds of chemo, the radiation portion of the process began. I had radiation every monday through Friday. Through radiation I worked the first half of every day, and had radiation every afternoon.

During radiation, I sat still on a body mold for 15 to 20 minutes while a huge donut machine worked its magic. With every session my pelvis and my lower back ached more and more.

In addition too work, I was also earning my MBA during my cancer treatment.

Throughout this process I heard from family, friends, acquinatances, customers, co workers all sending prayers, gifts and healing energy.

The prayers and love I received were instrumental in my survival. I will forever be grateful for the love I received. It's reciprocated.

After chemo and radiation, and so many bodily reactions, I was happy to hear that the tumor had amazingly almost completely vanished. However, there could be microscopic cancer cells there if left untreated. In March of 2023, I had a resection surgery. where that section of the digestive system was removed. I was given a temporary ileostomy bag. It was gross, uncomfortable, but I was still grateful as it was better than cancer.

Due to complications, I stayed in the hospital for eleven days.

I had an ileostomy bag on my 50th birthday. I went to a restaurant with my friends. Blanca was so kind to coordinate the event. I was grateful, but I did not feel like myself. I felt weak and barely ate. Blanca and all my friends there that night are my angels. A small group of strong women guided by love and faith.

In May 2023, I had the ileostomy reversal surgery and the bag was finally removed.

I had no evidence of disease which is fantastic, but I did have LARS or lower anterior resection syndrome. Basically the symptoms are the constant urge to have a bowel movement. Going to the bahroom often, usually within 30 minutes of consuming food. At this point, I was used to wearing diapers if I needed to leave the home, or fasting to avoid the need to go to the bathroom.

In December of 2023, I had my first CT Scan since my surgery, and everything was clear.

Throughout my cancer journey, I relied in many chats and forums of people battling the same things. I learned that GLP1 medications were slowing down the digestive system and alleviating the symptoms of LARS. Today, I am on Mounjaro and not only have I been able to shed some pounds, I have alleviated my LARS and my system almost works like it did before cancer. I am not a Doctor, and do not give any medical advice. This is my journey and everyone should consult with their doctors for their situations. Speaking of doctors I would like to thank my team of oncologists, surgeons and nurses at Memorial Healthcare, they saved my life.

CHAPTER 9

MBA

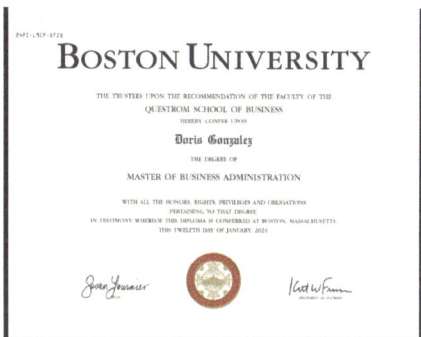

BU MBA Diploma

While earning my MBA I was working and battling cancer. I am happy to say that in January of 2024 I earned my Diploma. In May 2024, I will participate in the commencement ceremonies at Boston University, one year after my last cancer surgery.

Earning an MBA is meaningful for most students. But doing so while being the primary breadwinner in a household, and battling a cancer aggressively with debilitating chemotherapy, radiation and two surgeries in a 60 day time-span is mind blowing.

Sharing my story has helped family members and friends. I have helped to save lives. I hope that by sharing my story I will continue to help bring awareness to colonoscopies, and to know that each journey is unique.

While at school, I met so many intersting people. Each with amazing life experiences from a global perspective. I learned just as much from the other students as I did from the wonderful faculty. I am so proud of this accomplishment, and grateful to Boston University.

Lessons

Chapter Ten- Lessons

Faith- It doesn't matter what religion speaks to you. But it's important to have faith in a higher power. I believe in God. I have seen miracles and I am grateful. Being patient, doing the best you can, and letting go of control has been very helpful to me. The power of prayer is undeniable.

Tribe- Pick your tribe. Be there for them, and they will be there for you. I would not be here today if it wasn't for my tribe. My core, my family and my friends are my reason for being here. I am so grateful for all of them. They are a blessing. Align yourself with those with similar values.

Tribe

Mindset- Listen to your gut. Know your worth. If others won't see your worth, make it impossible for them not to notice. Don't be a victim. Throughout my life, there were many opportunities for me to be miserable and be a victim. Instead I stood tall, and fought with love and patience.

Have Fun- I work a lot. I have been through a lot. But I make sure that I am having fun throughout my journey. Whether it's short weekend trips with my husband, brunches with my friends, spending a couple hours at the beach, or full fledge vacations with people I care about. Balance is critical.

Always be learning- This is my first self published book. Will I get everything right? Of course not, but I tried, and I am learning, and I am sure if I do it again it will be better.

Never give up on your goals- Allow your self to dream and have lofty goals. Act on your dreams, no matter how small the step. Martin

Luther King stated you don't have to see the whole staircase, you only have to see the next step.

Don't take the easiest route- Sometimes the best outcomes come from busting your butt, and going through it with grit and perseverance.

Live each moment- Someone once said, the past is gone, the future is not promised, this moment is all their is. After the cancer battle, I appreciate each moment even more. I live intentionally, and choose peace, love and gratitude.

Chapter Ten- Lessons

Faith- It doesn't matter what religion speaks to you. But it's important to have faith in a higher power. I believe in God. I have seen miracles and I am grateful. Being patient, doing the best you can, and letting go of control has been very helpful to me. The power of prayer is undeniable.

Tribe- Pick your tribe. Be there for them, and they will be there for you. I would not be here today if it wasn't for my tribe. My core, my family and my friends are my reason for being here. I am so grateful for all of them. They are a blessing. Align yourself with those with similar values.

Tribe

Mindset- Listen to your gut. Know your worth. If others won't see your worth, make it impossible for them not to notice. Don't be a victim. Throughout my life, there were many opportunities for me to be miserable and feel like a victim. Instead I stood tall, and fought with love and patience.

Have Fun- I work a lot. I have been through a lot. But I make sure that I am having fun throughout my journey. Whether it's short weekend trips with my husband, brunches with my friends, spending a couple hours at the beach, or full fledge vacations with people I care about. Balance is critical.

Always be learning- This is my first self published book. Will I get everything right? Of course not, but I tried, and I am learning, and I am sure if I do it again it will be better.

Never give up on your goals- Allow yourself to dream and have lofty goals. Act on your dreams, no matter how small the step. Martin Luther King stated you don't have to see the whole staircase, you only have to see the next step.

Don't take the easiest route- Sometimes the best outcomes come from busting your butt, and going through it with grit and perseverance.

Live each moment- Someone once said, the past is gone, the future is not promised, this moment is all there is. After the cancer battle, I appreciate each moment even more. I live intentionally, and choose peace, love and gratitude.

www.ingramcontent.com/pod-product-compliance
Lightning Source LLC
Chambersburg PA
CBHW040905120626
46551CB00006B/655